P9-CQW-936

Coffee Talk
A Nano Sized
Teambuilding Game

By
Tyler Hayden

www.tylerhayden.com

Coffee Talk
A Nano Sized
Teambuilding Game

Copyright © Tyler Hayden, 2005, 2009

All rights reserved. The use of any part of this publication reproduced, transmitted in any form or by any means, electronic, mechanical, recorded, or otherwise, or stored in retrieval systems, without the prior written permission of the publisher is an infringement on the copyright.

Published by Tyler Hayden,
P.O. Box 604
Mahone Bay, Nova Scotia
Canada
B0J 2E0

Illustrations: Ken Lepage
Cover Design: Kathryn Marcellino
Interior Design: Dennis Marcellino
Printed and bound in USA through Lightning Source

National Library of Canada Cataloguing in Publication
Hayden, Tyler, 1974–
    Coffee Talk : a nano sized teambuilding game / Tyler Hayden.
ISBN   978-1-897050-08-8
    1. Business.   2. Games.   3. Special Interest.   I. Title.

I dedicate this book to
all the coffee shops in the world.
Thank you for the sweets, free internet and
clean bathrooms –
not to mention injections of caffeine...

Coffee Talk©

Building a strong relationship within your staff is a cornerstone to a great organization. And there is no better way to do this then by having a little Coffee Talk©.

Coffee Talk© is an interactive teambuilding activity that happens between two to six people. And the beautiful part of the activity is that it is so simple to do that all you need is a copy of Coffee Talk©, a cup of Java, and some people to talk with.

For more information on Coffee Talk©, other great teambuilding products, and high-energy keynotes visit www.tylerhayden.com. Enjoy the Coffee Talk©!

Coffee
Talk ©

Pause
Conversation ©

How to Play

1. Invite some folks to gather together (at a staff meeting, retreat, or informally in the lunch room) and ask them if they would like to take a 15-minute break.
2. Pull out a copy of Coffee Talk© and explain how to play the game.
   a. Everyone grabs a coffee (or beverage of their choice) and sits around a table or in a circle.
   b. One person will be chosen to be the Coffee Talk reader.
   c. This person will open the book to a random coffee talk page and read the question out loud.
   d. Everyone takes turns going first and will have the opportunity to answer the question. (A fun variation is to encourage the group to ask questions about the person's response for even more depth and understanding.)
   e. If someone doesn't want to answer that question, they have the *right to pass* and not answer, in which case the turn goes to the next person.
   f. Play Coffee Talk© as long as time permits.

Coffee Talk ©

Pause Conversation ©

www.tylerhayden.com

The best attribute I bring to this team is…

Le meilleur attribut que j'apporte à cette
équipe est…

My Mom taught me…

Ma mère m'a appris…

Where do you go to relax? Why is that
the place you choose?

Où allez-vous pour vous détendre?
Pourquoi choisissez-vous cet endroit?

Coffee
Talk ©

Pause
Conversation ©

www.tylerhayden.com

The best skill I bring to this team is…

La meilleure compétence que j'apporte à cette équipe est…

I am most motivated when…

Je suis très motivé lorsque…

What is one thing that your parents were right about, but you hate to admit that they were right?

Citez un point sur lequel vos parents avaient raison et pour lequel vous avez des difficultés à admettre qu'ils avaient raison?

What are your thoughts on UFO's and extraterrestrial life forms?

Que pensez-vous des OVNIs et des formes de vie extraterrestre?

What is your greatest success
so far in life?

Quelle est la plus grande réussite de votre
vie jusqu'à maintenant?

If I could have dinner with one famous person (alive or dead) it would be…

Si je pouvais dîner en tête à tête avec une célébrité (vivante ou non), ce serait…

www.tylerhayden.com

What is your all time favorite movie?
Why?

Quel est votre film favori? Pourquoi?

Coffee
Talk ©

Pause
Conversation ©

What is the most important thing in your life right now? Why?

Quelle est la chose la plus importante dans votre vie actuelle? Pourquoi?

Coffee Talk ©

Pause Conversation ©

My greatest hero or heroine is…
because…

Mon plus grand héros ou ma plus grande
héroïne est…parce que…

Coffee Talk ©

Pause Conversation ©

The thing I'm looking forward to the most about working with this team is…

La tâche de mon travail que j'ai le plus hâte d'accomplir avec cette équipe est…

What is one thing people wouldn't know about you, that would be surprising, that you would like to share?

Quelle chose aimeriez-vous partager à votre sujet et qui surprendrait les gens?

Who is your favorite musician?

Qui est votre musicien favori?

If you could stop one world crisis, which one would it be? Why?

Si vous pouviez faire cesser une crise mondiale qui se produit actuellement, laquelle choisiriez-vous et pourquoi?

www.tylerhayden.com

Who is your greatest role model?

Qui est votre plus grand modèle?

The best thing that happened to me this week is…

La meilleure chose qui m'est arrivé cette semaine est…

My family is…

Ma famille est…

If I could do another job other than the one I am currently in I would love to…

Si je pouvais occuper un autre emploi que l'actuel, j'aimerais…

Coffee **Talk**©

Pause **Conversation** ©

What is your fondest memory of your
children or of when you were a child?

Quel est votre meilleur souvenir de vos
enfants ou de votre enfance?

Coffee
Talk ©

Pause
Conversation ©

My Dad taught me…

Mon père m'a appris…

How do you think they got the caramel
inside the Caramilk Bar?

D'après vous, comment met-on le caramel
dans la barre Caramilk?

If you could have one 'do-over' in life,
what would it be?

Si vous pouviez recommencer une chose
dans la vie, quelle serait-elle?

What do you see yourself doing two years from now?

Quelle chose vous voyez-vous faire dans deux ans?

My dream vacation is…

Mes vacances de rêve sont…

If you could bronze a part of your body what part would you choose and why?

Si vous pouviez couler dans le bronze une partie de votre corps, laquelle choisiriez-vous et pourquoi?

Coffee
Talk ©

Pause
Conversation ©

www.tylerhayden.com

What is the most "off the wall, spur of the moment" thing you have ever done?

Quelle est la chose la plus inusitée et spontanée que vous ayez jamais faite?

My greatest strength is…

Ma plus grande force est…

My favourite part of my job is…

L`aspect de mon travail que
je prefere est…

My favorite possession is…

La chose préférée que je possède est…

I eat Chunky soup with a …
(fork or spoon)

Je mange ma soupe Chunky avec une…
(fourchette ou cuillère)

What holiday do you go all out for (i.e.: Halloween, Valentine's Day, etc)?

Quelle fête vous engage à fond (c.-à-d., Halloween, Saint-Valentin, etc.)?

The one thing I hate to do at work is…

La chose que je déteste faire
au travail est…

If you won $10 Million what would you
do with it?

Si vous gagniez 10 millions de dollars,
qu'en feriez-vous?

What is your greatest passion?

Quelle est votre plus grande passion?

What is the most life defining moment for
you in your life so far?

Quel a été le moment le plus déterminant
de votre vie?

My kids taught me…

Mes enfants m'ont appris…

What is your favorite saying or quote?

Quel est votre dicton ou citation favori?

What is your favorite TV show? Why?

Quelle est votre émission de télé favorite? Pourquoi?

If you could be on one reality TV show, which one would it be? Why?

Si vous pouviez participer à une émission de télé-réalité, laquelle choisiriez-vous et pourquoi?

Coffee
Talk©

Pause
Conversation ©

What are your 3 major goals
for right now?

Quels sont actuellement vos
3 grands buts?

What is your favorite game to play?

À quel jeu préférez-vous jouer?

What is the one thing that just gets on your nerves?

Quel chose vous tombe royalement sur les nerfs?

What has been your biggest challenge in
life that you have been able to overcome?

Quel à été le plus grand défi que vous
ayez pu surmonter dans votre vie?

www.tylerhayden.com

Who is the most famous person you have ever met? Or who is the most famous person you are friends with?

Quelle est la personne la plus célèbre que vous ayez rencontrée? Ou qui est la personne la plus célèbre de votre cercle d'amis?

Coffee Talk ©

Pause Conversation ©

What is the coolest place
you have ever visited?

Quel est l'endroit le plus génial que
vous ayez visité?

If you could blow $1000 on anything, what would you spend it on?

Si vous pouviez dépenser 1000$ pour n'importe quoi, que choisiriez-vous?

Coffee
Talk ©

Pause
Conversation ©

The greatest reward or recognition that I like to receive for a job well done is…

La plus grande récompense ou reconnaissance que j'aime recevoir pour un travail bien fair est…

Currently I volunteer my time for the…

Actuellement, je fais du
bénévolat pour…

What qualities do you respect and admire
in people the most?

Quelle qualité respectez-vous et admirez-
vous le plus chez les gens?

The weirdest thing I've ever
purchased is…

La chose le plus bizarre que j'aie jamais
achetée est…

In my "free time" I like to…

Dans mes temps libres, j'aime…

What is your favourite way to spend your
time after work or on your weekends?

Quel est votre passe-temps favori après le
travail ou les fins de semaine?

What make of car best describes
your personality?

Quelle marque de voiture décrit le mieux
votre personnalité?

If I could have dinner with one famous person (alive or dead) it would be…

Si je pouvais dîner en tête à tête avec une célébrité (vivante ou non), ce serait…

Coffee Talk ©

Pause Conversation ©

Have a burning question that you'd like to ask? That's cool. Go ahead and write it here for the next time you play Coffee Talk.

_____

_____

_____

Have a burning question that you'd like to ask? That's cool. Go ahead and write it here for the next time you play Coffee Talk.

_____

_____

_____

Have a burning question that you'd like to ask? That's cool. Go ahead and write it here for the next time you play Coffee Talk.

_____

_____

_____

Coffee
Talk©

Pause
Conversation ©

www.tylerhayden.com

Have a burning question that you'd like to ask? That's cool. Go ahead and write it here for the next time you play Coffee Talk.

_____

_____

_____

Have a burning question that you'd like to ask? That's cool. Go ahead and write it here for the next time you play Coffee Talk.

_____

_____

_____

Coffee
Talk ©

Pause
Conversation ©

www.tylerhayden.com

Have a burning question that you'd like to ask? That's cool. Go ahead and write it here for the next time you play Coffee Talk.

_____

_____

_____

Have a burning question that you'd like to ask? That's cool. Go ahead and write it here for the next time you play Coffee Talk.

_____

_____

_____

Have a burning question that you'd like to ask? That's cool. Go ahead and write it here for the next time you play Coffee Talk.

_____

_____

_____

Have a burning question that you'd like to ask? That's cool. Go ahead and write it here for the next time you play Coffee Talk.

_____

_____

_____

Coffee
Talk ©

Pause
Conversation ©

Have a burning question that you'd like to ask? That's cool. Go ahead and write it here for the next time you play Coffee Talk.

_____

_____

_____

Have a burning question that you'd like to ask? That's cool. Go ahead and write it here for the next time you play Coffee Talk.

_____

_____

_____

Pause
Conversation ©

www.tylerhayden.com

Caution:
The following pages contain shameless advertising of more fun team building activities by Tyler!

More Great Teambuilding Activities

Talk-a-lote Pizzeria Board Game

This game is an absolute blast to play with a team that is between 4 and 14 members. It is easy to learn to play, you won't break a sweat, doesn't take any special skills, cooperative in nature, and one of the best ways to get people talking with each other.

The game is based on the table game "quarters" where one individual bounces a quarter off the table and if it lands in the plate that is sitting on the table the group must perform a task, in our case answer a question from one of the six stacks of questions. Teams get to know each other easily as dialogue quickly opens up about questions like, "Would you rather, be the lead singer for an ABBA or AC/DC cover band?" And, which would you rather do and why "Be Darth Vader or Luke Skywalker?" With over 300 important questions like that – this game is a great way to open dialogue and get to know your team a bit better.

Full game includes: a pizza plate, painted bottle caps, bag, quarter, cards, score sheet, rules, all in a pizza box!

This is definitely a great tool for any manager or trainer to have in their toolbox for an upcoming meeting, retreat or training event.

Buy it online at: www.tylerhayden.com

Team Suite One and Two

Team Suite One's CD ROM is jam packed with ready to use teambuilding activities. You will be able to have interesting, fun and ready to go team activities for your next meeting. This Team Suite contains these fantastic team development activities:

> **Scavenger Hunter** – various 15 minute Scavenger Hunts custom designed for Hotels, Cars, Brief Cases, and more. This challenge comes complete with a countdown clock and ready to print sheets. All you have to do is bring the people!

> **Commonalities** – This is a quick warm up/get to know you event that pits table against table to see who is the most alike! Great fun, and truly explains the adage "truth is stranger than fiction!"

> **Last Call** – This too is a quick get to know you/ ice breaker elimination game. Individuals will be pitted against each other to see who won't miss "Last Call."

I Like You Because... – Often times we don't say what we mean, and even rarer still do we write it down. This fantastic recognition event has us do the later. You'll see smiles from ear to ear on participants at the conclusion of this event; it's one of Tyler's favourites!

Fact or Fiction – This is an awesome team trivia competition. It takes a bit of set up on your part, in both prep and implementation – but you'll experience a low cost, high impact get to know the team event with this one. This event can last 30 to 40 minutes or be used progressively throughout your meeting day. Tons of fun.

There were so much fun team events we couldn't fit them on just one CD ROM, hence the birth of Team Suite Two. Check out these innovative team building activities:

Light It UP – One of Tyler's most engaged team events. You're going to love "playing this game at home." You'll get all the templates you need and the content generators for this high energy, and often hilarious event. You get the whole package... well except you'll need to find your own host because like batteries – Tyler's not included.

Thoughts on Fire – About to do some problem solving or planning at your next meeting. Then this activity is for you. This slide show is jam packed with engaging brain teasers that will get your team's brains pumping on all cylinders, and quick.

Situation Room – This is a fantastic group of creative thinking experiences. Your team will be given a problem to solve. They will then begin to creatively find solutions. But the event doesn't stop there – there are twists and turns that will really get their pencils sharpened.

4 Corners – This is a fast and furious event. In 10 minutes your team will categorize themselves based on their preferences and see who else on the team shares their likes. This is a quick and fun way to break the ice with almost any group.

Coffee Talk – This is a great way to get people taking. Tyler is a fan of "no breaks" during a team event. So one of the tools he built for coffee breaks was "Coffee Talk" the most entertaining little book you've ever read with someone else. This happens to be the electronic version... a fantastic way to spend a bit of a break!

Buy it online at: www.tylerhayden.com

About the Author

Tyler Hayden has been a full-time professional speaker and innovative educator for over a decade. His business is personal development and non-traditional team-building programs. Tyler's clients include some of the world's largest corporations like Scotiabank, Manulife, and Caterpillar and associations, like the Young Presidents Organization (YPO).

Tyler is a keynoter, team-builder and author. He has developed program solutions for groups in areas of leadership, management, teambuilding, staff motivation, HR Solutions, personal development, and soft skill development. He is the author of 16 books, 2 audio CDs, an 3 interactive CD ROMs, and a full-length DVD. His training materials have been sold worldwide, and he has delivered hundreds of high-energy keynotes and team-building programs.

Tyler balances his busy speaking career with two other business ventures -- Message in a Bottle Book Series, and HR Consulting -- both of which provide business and life solutions in innovative ways.

All work and no play? No way! Tyler enjoys travelling and experiencing new cultures and high-adrenaline activities, like skydiving, canyoning and survival camping. Tyler spends some of his "free" time at home renovating his family's 250-year old Cape Cod home and building folk art sculptures and paintings.

Finally, a description of Tyler would not be complete without a word about his greatest source of affluence: family. Tyler is a loving husband to Laurie, a high school principal, and proud father of Tait and Breton, his beautiful little girls. Tyler and Laurie look forward to building a loving family and continuing to make a difference in the quiet seaside community of Mahone Bay, Nova Scotia.

Tyler invites you to join him on a magnificent journey of Livin' Life Large™!

Learn more about Tyler's interactive Teambuilding and Keynote services at **www.tylerhayden.com**.

LaVergne, TN USA
19 January 2010
170400LV00004B/2/P

9 781897 050088